Child of War

Child of War

Poems by Genny Lim

2003

Library of Congress Catalog Card Number: 2003106647
ISBN: 0-9709597-3-7

Kalamaku Press
1710 Punahou Street, Apt. 601
Honolulu, HI 96822

Printed in the USA.

Cover Photos:

Varanasi, India: The ancient city of Varanasi sits on the banks of the sacred Ganges. One dip in the sacred waters is said to purify all negative karma. The long row of ghats lead down to the river, where pilgrims bathe at dawn in the "elixir of life." Smoke rises constantly from the burning ghats, where bodies are cremated.

Bamiyan, Afghanistan: The giant statue of Buddha sculpted in a sandstone cliff of the Hindu Kush was considered the most remarkable representation of the Buddha anywhere in the world. The statue stood at 53 metres (125 feet)—as high as a 10-story building. In March 2001, the Taliban dynamited the statue, because "all statues were false idols and contrary to their Islamic beliefs."

Acknowledgements

Colette Jue, the best sister, friend and daughter anyone could ever have; Cecilia Lim, for being there; Herbie Lewis, a true friend and one of the greatest bass players in America; the late Marijane Lee, for making us laugh; Dennis Kawaharada, for his support in publishing this book; and The Three Jewels.

Dedicated to Danielle Mai Ting Jue

May 16, 1982 – September 9, 2001

Fireflies

I find it quite amazing how the people
who sometimes make the most impact on your life
are the ones who pass through briefly.
They remind me of fireflies.
Winking by, teasing with their soft glowing bodies,
you run after them to try and capture the light they give off,
but before you know it, the sun rises, and
the glittering bugs have disappeared.
The sad fact is you don't realize the fireflies' soft, magical beauty
until they are gone
because you were too busy trying to capture them.

Journal entry by Danielle Jue

Contents

I

II

III

IV

Epilogue

/

Lullabye for Danielle

She won't allow me to sing
And how I love to sing!
The moment I croon
Her round face wilts and
Her eyes brim over
Like two floating black marbles

If I swoop her into my arms
If I tattoo kisses on her lips, the nape of her neck
If I devour her cheeks and nose like raspberries
If I pinch her toes
Will she recoil?

I place her tiny tapered feet on my palms
How small, how delicate
The way the pink toes curl under, like fuchsia petals!
Sadly, they make me think of bound feet
Mothers, take heed, and listen to your lullabyes!

Children are Color-Blind

I never painted myself yellow
The way I colored the sun when I was five
The way I colored white-folks with the flesh crayola
Yellow pages adults thumbed through for restaurants, taxis,
        airlines, plumbers . . .
The color of summer squash, corn,
                egg-yolk, innocence and tapioca

My children knew before they were taught
They envisioned rainbows over alleyways
Clouds floating over hilltops like a freedom-shroud
With hands held, time dragged them along and they followed

Wind-flushed cheeks, persimmon
Eyes dilated like dark pearls, peering from backseat windows
Like greyhounds, they sped through childhood into
The knot of night, hills fanning out
Ocean ending at an underpass
The horizon blurring

Dani, my three-year old, recites the alphabet
From billboards flashing by like pages of a cartoon flip-book
Where above, carpetbaggers patrol the freeways like
Olympic gods hustling their hi-tech neon gospel
Looking down from the fast lane
Dropping Kool dreams, booze dreams, fancy car dreams
Fast foods dreams, sex dreams and no-tomorrow dreams
Like eight balls into your easy psychic pocket

Only girls with black hair, black eyes can join!
My eight year old was chided at school for
Excluding a blonde from her circle
Only girls with black hair, black eyes can join!
Taunted the little Asian girls.

Black hair, black eyes flashing, mirroring,
        mimicking what they heard
As the message of the medium
The message of the world-at-large
Apartheid, segregation, self-determination!
Segregation, apartheid, revolution!
Like a contrapuntal hymn, like a curse that refrains in
A melody trapped

Sometimes at night, I touch the children when they're sleeping
And the coolness of my fingers
        sends shivers through them that is
A foreshadowing, a guilt imparted

Dani doesn't paint herself yellow
They way I colored the sun
She dances in its light as I watch from the shadow
No, she says, green is her favorite color
It's the color of life!

Dani's Finches

They hatched
those tiny, perfectly oval, perfectly white eggs
Each one, a trembling, outburst of life
Five pebble-sized heads, twisting slowly
like fuzzy pink marbles
Hungry, wide open beaks pecking through
the shell of past lives
You beam, at the awestruck little zebra finches
Like some proud magician,
who conjured life on the tips of your fingers
in an instant

Turning of the Page

In memory of Danielle

The story unfolds with a beautiful young girl
Who made people laugh, who loved life and smiled
She was charmed and could tease the leaves off the trees
She wasn't bad at fixing things either and
Could whip a stereo set together or
assemble a piece of furniture in record time
while her mother stood scratching her head
What can't she do? Her mother wondered
As her daughter carried the brand new 17-inch Sony
down the street and up two flights to the apartment by herself
As she watched TV, did her homework
        and chatted on the phone and still got straight A's?
She had it all
Friends, family, influence
A confident genius, whose only passion it seemed was
to be happy and to make others happy
Everyone loved her, everyone admired her
A perfect girl, her sister said, in every way
Most stories have a beginning, middle and end
This story, however, does not
Without twists, turns or plot
The page is stuck
While time keeps turning
Like leaves blown off the ground of memory
And the theme
What is it really?
If not a moment fully lived, fully loved
Fully touched?

Just Now

Just now you are waking in the Bardo
Wandering the empty streets of the mind
Do not be afraid of the spirits who greet you
The Wrathful Herukas and Guaris who arise
They are the terrifying messengers of the Five Buddhas
Who open the gates for you

I will make burnt offerings for your safe journey
Fragrant incense smoke from Bhutan
Carefully gathered in the gentle breeze of
alpine meadows under the full moon
Plants and herbs containing the precious essences of heaven
and mountain earth baked in sunlight to guide your way
Saffron water will quench your thirst and roasted tsampa with
The three white and three sweet ingredients will fill your senses
With the lost pleasures of the body

No tears! warns Garchin Rinpoche
Or you might cling to Samsara
Better to chant the Mani and let you go your way
The amrita of pure awareness awaits you and the
Honored guests at your table are anxious to meet you
But I will not be there to greet you, my sweetheart
To nag you to take along a sweater or extra cash
No, I will not be there to ask you who's driving and
What time will you be home

How difficult it is to let go of what we hold most dear
How difficult it is to shed your smile for all of time
More precious than life itself was the gift of your love to me
More precious than breath itself was the miracle of your life
So boundless with compassion yet so limited in span
Yes I was attached to you
That was my downfall
So now the cord is cut

You often asked me why I stared
I was drawn like a moth to the warmth of your smile
Your self-assurance came freely
So young, so beautiful, so natural
You knew the shortcut to Nirvana
Without arduous retreats
Your yearbook quote,
"Once you're capable of taking in the water,
you don't mind the coming and going of the waves . . ."

They said you floated
Arms raised above your head, perfectly serene
Your face shrouded in the halo of afternoon light
Down, down stream you floated on your back
Arms high above your head
Eyes shut
Dreaming

Om Gate Gate Parasamgate Bodhi Soha

The Bardo Thödol has been recited one hundred times
By the monks at Drepung Löseling all the way in India
Sur Offerings have been made twice a day for two weeks
The Naydren ceremony has completed the 49-day Bardo cyle
Now may you rest in eternal peace and joy
Yesterday we made 108 tsa-tsas for you
Tiny clay stupas containing your ashes were
floated out to sea at sunset
We caravaned to the marina at Fort Mason
Took pictures as if to save you a shot
Then trudged all over to find the perfect spot
At the tip of the Wave Organ
Everyone marveled at the beauty of the bay
It was the Day of Mahasamadhi, the Divine Mother
And the night of the meteor showers
I filled the ti leaf boats with the tiny clay stupas
And waited as Dennis, who watched you blossom
from child to young woman
climb down to the edge of the rocks to
gently place each boat into the icy current
The rock organ was silent that evening and
Our group of fifteen seemed to hold its breath together
As the tsa-tsas tumbled into the sea
Vanishing instantly as they touched water
We had imagined them floating out on the tide
But they were swallowed up before
We could even take a breath
We sighed when the last boat disappeared
Then headed back to our cars
Om Gate, Gate …
How simple it is to take a breath
Om Gate, Gate, Parasamgate, Bodhi Soha
How difficult to hold it

Animal Liberation

Other than a chickadee which I had bought from
a pick-up truck vendor many, many years ago
I had never purchased a live animal
Today I went to Chinatown and parked on the south end of Grant
I walked down the street
       combing the poultry shops for a live duck
Most of the old markets had been shut down
under pressure from the Animal Humane Society
No more cages piled high on the sidewalks with the odor of fowl
or loose feathers dusting the already acrid air
Wooden crates jammed with roosters, hens and pigeons
Barrels of live frogs and turtles had been replaced by
Spanking new tourist emporiums spilling silk brocades
Chinaware and hand-carved deities from over-stocked shelves
I make my way through the crowds into one market displaying
Roasted ducks hanging upside-down
I ask the proprietress, "Do you have any live ducks?"
She points next door
I walk into a long, narrow room
       with wooden cages kept behind a glass partition
"Do you have any live ducks?"
       I ask the old poker-faced poultry man
Without blinking, he asks, "How many?"
I ask him, "How much for one?" in Chinese
He answers, "Sup-yih-gah-bun!"
Twelve dollars and fifty-cents for the life of a duck?
I reply, "One!"
He turns around and opens the door to one of the crates
and reaches in and pulls out a big, speckled brown duck
He grabs it by the neck and ties its feet together
Then he stuffs the bird into a paper bag
       punctured with holes at the top
I pay him my money and he hands over the bag

I am so excited my heart is racing all the way out the door
I clutch the duck's warm body against my chest and
It feels like that of my baby
        before she had grown into a beautiful young lady
Hard to believe nineteen years had passed since
I had held her tiny body to me just like this
I walk the length of Grant Avenue with my contraband
I'm relieved I don't have a ticket
        and place the duck in the back of the car
I head out to the park with a heightened awareness
        of my sudden new surroundings
The buildings are unusually vivid, the pedestrians unusually alive
I park at Stow Lake and walk around till I find
a spot near the reeds obscured from view
I walk down the embankment with my heart throbbing
I open the bag half expecting the duck to bite me
But she sits there calmly and patiently and as I untie
the tight band of wire wrapped around her legs
Talking to her gently as I free her
I'm afraid to upset her by picking her up so
I turn the bag upside down and literally pour her into the water
She tumbles into the lake and
        as soon as her body makes contact with liquid
There is instant recognition
She dives into the pool and emerges
        with her feathers wet and glistening
She spreads her wings wide for the first time and quacks with joy
She dives in and out again and again
Baptizing her entire body with miraculous water
My heart sings to see this once captive duck
Frolic in the lake, diving and dancing, flapping her wings
as flocks of black guinea hens pass by in cool demeanor
And proud mallards observe their new member
        with calm disinterest
She quacks and cavorts like a prisoner released from death row

I sigh, never taking my eyes off her for a moment
Until she is joined by an identical speckled brown duck
They swim together past the boaters, past the reeds beyond sight
"Free!" I breathe, "at last!"
One life saved for another one lost
Good-bye my darling, Danielle!
May your consciousness leap
        into the vast and familiar depths of Sukhavati
And may you reunite quickly
        with the hosts of enlightened beings
Who have gone on ahead of you and who will soon follow!

Missing you

I miss the form that was you
the smooth skin that was you
the scent of peaches that was you
the shiny black hair that was you
the laughter that was you
the warmth that was you
the smile that was you
the fast tongue that was you
the good times that was you
the good food that was you
the soft hands that was you
the slender hips that was you
the tender lips that was you
the round face that was you
the perfect nose that was you
the gleaming white teeth that was you
the almond eyes that was you
the gliding stroll that was you
the fashions that was you
the ringing cell phone and I-M that was you
the countless friends that was you
the cussing that was you
the wit that was you
the song that was you
the world that was you
the rain that is now you
the empty house that is now you
the silence that is now you
the absence that is now you
the me without you

No Greater Love

When the noise stops
there's just the scent of apples
to remember your skin by
When the bickering's over
the endless litany of who did what to whom and
what went wrong stops
there is only a ribbon of moonlight
to trace your smile in the dark
When the crescendoing rage of
seeing you in the rapid all alone with
your foot bound to a rock in tragic metaphor
there is just your laughter rippling
over the edge like a nonsense waterfall
When the pain of your absence looms
there is the small consolation of your innocence spared
from the terrors of a world at war
When sorrow weighs like a stone
there is just the echo of your voice ricocheting off the walls,
sidewalks, streets and rooftops
        to quell my grief and answer me
Why?
Why is there no greater love than the one that's lost?
The one that keeps growing long after death?

This Woman's Work

Christmas day.
Gray morning. Gray mourning.
My mind is a cloud.
It covers like a shroud, my Beautiful Sky.
This first Christmas without you, my sweetheart, is so lonely
Where are the presents, which used to stack up against the tree?
The scent of cinnamon, eucalyptus and pine?
A few unopened packages adorn the foot of the altar.
I sit in the permanent chill of your room,
warmed only now by the frozen smiles of happier times.
Prom dresses and fancy upswept hairdos,
stuffed bears and dogs of all colors, shapes and sizes,
a wall poster of your favorite hip hop artists,
another of baby angels floating on clouds overhead.
Class of 2000, lifetime member of Shield and Scroll,
California Scholarship Federation, Freshman Dean's Honor List . . .
Where it all stopped.
And the successes became memorabilia over night.
A hollow crown for a once story book Chinese American home-girl
Home-girl, where have u gone 2?
We listen to the cuts you burned before they were even released
You were always ahead of everybody else
Oh pray God, you can cope,
This woman's work, This woman's world . . .
I should be crying but I just can't let it show. . .
Oh darling, make it go, make it go away . . .
Give me these moments back. . .
Maxwell's voice rises in trembling falsetto
This woman's work, this woman's world, this grief, this burden,
This mother who carries her masterpiece on her back
which "No one should ever have to endure!" said Ani Kunzang
We brought orchids, anthuriums and cyclamen to
a grave of fresh red marble, a headstone without a face
to commemorate the beauty that lies beneath

Colette brought you a wreath with three pine cones
We bowed to you my dear
You were the first to cross over
It's not that you were never afraid
It was because you were always the most brave
The rose that grew from concrete,
The bloom love crafted.

Yama

My tears fall into Yama's lap and
dissolve into bygone memories
You're always appearing just out of reach
like the sun dropping below the ocean
You were in the middle of arranging for lodging
I found a box of candles and a shiny new black wallet
inside a bag for William's birthday
The brochures and map of Yosemite
the list of rental cars and hotels are still on your table
near your bed where you left them

The faded corsages and roses from your senior boat dance
Winter ball and proms still adorn your wall
A bevy of smiling young faces
        in elegant satin gowns and tuxedos
Surround you at its center like a rainbow
Your mementos and photo albums are everywhere
so numbered, precious and sweet
Each special occasion and event in a world fully inhabited and
a life fully spent and lovingly chronicled
We covet your photos like sacred relics
Your frozen image is our most valuable possession
Filling the silence of no more birthdays
A Thanksgivingless dinner and joyless Christmas
endured without you

The echo of your voice fills the rooms and
Mornings are greeted with a prisoner's gloom
Drifting memories crowd my thoughts
like vintage wine poured into a broken cup
Death comes and goes without reason or warning
It scoops up its chosen object, like a thief in the night
Leaving everything as if untouched
Yet defiling everything in sight

Echo

Just as you can never relive the past,
You can never relive love
No matter how vivid the memory or
How powerful the feeling,
The moment can never happen again
That is life's great sorrow
Attachment to things that change
If you've ever returned to a house you've left,
You will know how impossible,
How bereft, is your desire,
To sustain what's already been lost.
It's better not to return
to the uninhabited
It's best not to cling to shadows
It's best not to linger
Where no one lives,
Like an echo

Memorial Day

We filled the hole, each one of us
where your smile radiated without sadness or regret
above the blue ceramic Circle of Friendship you made
       in middle school and
               the firey torch ginger and birds of paradise
                   standing tall on your altar
With bright-colored origami cranes flitting across the walls and
pink and lavender baby anthuriums flown in fresh from Hawai'i,
pizzas, soda pop and Kwan Yin to commemorate your life
We filled the abcess,
       eating our hearts out with your favorite songs
We hug, shake hands, smile and pose in front of your artwork
as if the birthday party could go on year after year
with one more candle to add to the twenty
that cannot be lit without your warmth
       or blown out without your breath
We fill the hole with a silent meditation on emptiness
as the hollow ocean inside our hearts
       envelope the ache of your absence
as the rhythm of our lonely heartbeats syncopate with the bass
We fill the hole, each one of us, alone and together
because we are one community now, bound by your love
like strangers caught in an elevator whose doors will not open
Attired in clothes of mourning, Wayne is stoic and solemn,
Leeme, ashen and pale, Carey, quiet and sweet,
M-J, ever bodacious and cheery,
       singing, "You gotta accent the positive!"
We come out of loyalty, respect, love, fear and dread
in the resounding wail of Francis's horn
in one long, tremolo of grief, sweetened by the images of
your mischievous antics,
       amazing friendships and carefree moments
proudly narrated by your sister Colette

After everyone leaves,
        Herbie invokes your spirit with a bass eulogy of
melodies from around the world
disclosing to the handful left how
        you were only one among a few people
in the world he knew, who had that certain look,
        that special gift of openness
which only spiritual people
        like Joe Henderson and Harold Land had
And how strange it was that the three of you
        took off about the same time
You had that certain look when he first got to know you in 1991
It was during the Solar Eclipse
        at the Rufino Tamayo Museum in Mexico City
You were eleven and the day suddenly became pitch black
You got lost in the mad crowd and
I was panicked trying to find you in the darkness

                    May 27, 2002

Stolen Beauty

Rage is the python
which swallows the heart
I am the woman who makes no apology
Love and hate spring from me

A good woman bears her cross with humility
She is a paragon, a virgin of invisible flight
Her name is pity

If you cut open a frog
It will bleed to death
Everything inside will stop
But its muscles will contract
and its heart will continue to beat

Rage is the revenge of the heart and
I am the heart of Darkness
Durga's nemesis

Here and Now

You are here. Here and now.
Inside.
Where the relic of your smile lies buried.
Here. Inside the leaves.
Where the willow weeps all around you.
You are everywhere.
Dancing through the branches with the moon
Shimmering black hair, sparkling eyes, singing loud
Over there!
      Climbing among the tangled boughs across the Pacific
Lifting your arms to beckon the new year
You are here, inside the trunk of the grandfather tree
Where the man in the stetson hat searches
      for the missing grandmother
Among the ruins of secret loves, losses and betrayals
      so legend here
You, too, have found your way to the tree
Your slender body, no longer bound to the rope of mortality
You're as radiant as the full moon in the dumbstruck sky

Half Full

I keep pushing, pushing through space,
which keeps receding through time
My hands reach through a staircase
        which separates me from you
Just inches away, a quantum step above and below,
        a leap from behind
I see you so clearly
Your skin bright alabaster
Your black hair pulled back high from your forehead
The same rounded forehead
        I caressed and kissed a thousand times

We look at each other, face to face
Your eyes stare back at me like mirrors
You are naked and leaning over as if stepping into a bath
I reach to touch you but you recede from me
With arms outstretched, determined to reach you,
        I rush towards you
But you are falling, falling down through
        the abyss of I know not where
I want so badly to catch up with you,
        to hold you in my arms and tell you
I love you and struggle to say the words
        and force them out of my numb mouth
"Ah-ah-uh-oo!" I mumble through the dream
"Ah-ah-uh-oo!" I repeat, tearing through the thick eye of slumber
Trying desperately to push my body
        like a camel through the needle of emptiness
I want to be with you! I shout through my mind
I want to join you! I cry with all my might
She comprehends yet there is nothing she can do to
Break down the wall

Yesterday on the news I heard that a church in Los Altos with
an Arab American congregation
was burned to the ground by arson fire

A seventeen year old Palestinian girl
        blew herself up in the marketplace and
killed six Israelis, including a sixteen year old girl
And a family of four in a Contra Costa suburban home was
found dead in a murder suicide
I ask myself, Is the glass half empty or is the glass half full?
Is it the living who are dying or is it the dead who are living?
People are building panic rooms in their houses with steel walls
equipped with video cameras, lasers and guns
People who once feared death and who now fear life
who want to know, Are their lives half empty or half full?

The candle flickers
Its glowing flame sparks the same old question
Is the glass half empty or is the glass half full?
The mother gently pulls the caul over her child
The phoenix moon rises in the unborn sky
I count the days since your departure
        without warning or goodbye
When the river took you
And you slipped from the grip of time
Your future racing after you

Karma

How is one to view karma, I asked Baba Hariji yesterday,
when an innocent life comes to sudden death?
Some believe, he replied, when a person's karma is fulfilled
there is no more reason for them to stay on further
      so they just pass on.
They have fulfilled their purpose and it is time to go.

Like the blue jay I watched flash before my eyes
and vanish behind the branches of a tree
You flew past the window blind
leaving no trace behind
Like the note of a raga you faded into echo
Light shines for only moments at a time
We think the sun is passing behind clouds
but it is the clouds who conceal her
So like that, I think you appear and
try to cling to your shadow

If you cut off my finger, it will still always be there!
a young man once said to me.
I can never stop missing it.
I had only known him for a day and did not believe him.
Now I look everywhere and see that you are in fact still there
Shining, like the phantom moon hidden by day
I look in your room and you are seated in lotus position
on the computer chair, smiling just as always
Instant messages, you're sending to all your friends
Love songs and plans, whispered in the dark to Wayne
Your long plaid flannel body pillow is still molded
to the shape of your body
Sky-clad bird, you've left everything behind
Except your memory
So what are we to do with all your possessions?
When we don't have the courage like you
to leap off the branch and fly
into the face of our own fears?

The Killing Field

Somewhere a voice cries out
It is that of a child's, crying, Mommy, Mommy!
But not one child, it is the voice of many children.
If Lady Macbeth believed that all the perfumes of Arabia
could not erase the stain of one drop of blood,
then all the laughter, all the music, all the banners,
all the good intentions, all the poems in the world
cannot silence this one cry, this one moan,
      escaping earth's crack.
Who is this child,
      who cries from the desolation of a mother's womb?
Who is this child, whose tender flesh is
      betrayed by mortar shells? smart bombs?
Whose tiny bones crumble under the weight of army tanks?
Who is this child who is swallowed repeatedly by fear
      the way a feline mother consumes her young?
Can forgetfulness deceive death?
Does indifference make habit out of mourning?
Food for the lucky ones will indeed survive a run on coffins
But is there enough earth to cover the grief of one loss?
Let alone manicured plots for the countless dying?
Our collective sorrow is an empty killing field
a scaffolding of bones laid bare
beyond the universe of shame,
commemorating those, who no longer fear

Child of War

Be still, heart, let the bombs blast away 175-feet high
smashing your holy head!
Let your standing frame and legs shatter
under the weight of the Mighty Taliban's sword!
Allahu Akbar! God is great, you pray
And the mothers are weeping in the desert camps
Bone chilling winds make time stand still,
while the cold hands of a clock advance like an overlord

Be still, my heart, you cannot reverse the technology of hate
Nor can you reverse its tragic course,
from dawn to dust, city after city
A trailing corpse of memory,
a demented ghost chasing unending suffering
Bury the little ones with eyes their closed,
swaddled in dissolving clothes
Their phantom bones will never know
the plumpness of a well-fed childhood
or the gurgling infatuation of adolescent love
or a marriage with all that accompanies it
Madness, joy, sadness, grief, pride, hope and passion

The deserted caves of Tora Bora lie silent tonight
Once the target of U.S. soldiers combing through the rubble
for unused artillery and failed plots of sabotage
The scorched landscape has returned to the warlords
War has become the greatest commodity of all time
Baghdad explodes under the weight of two-thousand pound bombs
The burning streets, which in our minds had become mines
of subterranean subversion, catacombs of demonic machinations
Temples of terrorism erected to smash our American Dream
Between the Tigris and the Euphrates
What is left is the devastation of Eden
What is left of the apple is
The worm of civilization
Cradled in some dead hero's heart

How can I tell you that we failed to protect you, little ones?
Asleep from war, asleep from hatred, asleep from fear
Dream that dream, that you will awaken inside a cloud
With petals of light floating, floating away on a windhorse
Surrounded by turquoise waterfalls
and flowing streams whispering your name
Dream that mantras of peace and harmony echo in the air and
carry every living and non-living being
Dream that every speck of dust rides on love's syllable

      Om Mani Padma Hum
      Om Mani Padma Hum
      Om Mani Padma Hum

Forgive us, Angel of Mercy, champions of the downtrodden
Look how all the temples are cracked,
look how all the plaster deities
and offering bowls have been shattered
Our guardians have descended to ashes and museum dust
Yes, in our town even the dead live better than the living
The mausoleums in the cemetery atop Millionaire's Row
rise in Ionic majesty
and the columbarium stands sheathed in granite and marble
Solid and white as the day they were built,
unscorched by shame or sorrow

The Terrorist

For Rachel Corrie

The terrorist who lives among us is not you
The terrorist who lurks in the shadows of our crowded
      city streets is not me
He is not a demon with bulging eyes,
a twisted mouth full of dirt and
crooked teeth and fangs dripping with blood
The terrorist amongst us does not have a belly that
sags from the weight of innocent flesh consumed
He is not the savage gunner who waits for our children
to turn the corner on their way to school or
the mad monster itching to detonate a human bomb
No, this heinous, hateful replica of Satan does not look like
an Arab or Jew, Asian or Caucasian, Indian or African
Don't trouble yourself to look for the one who most resembles
the photograph or sketch of our televised enemy
Don't make a habit of supplying the motives of sin
      hidden underneath dark skin because
the enemy is skin deep
The enemy is the corner grocer with a family of four or
a pipe-fitter with a slain mother and child or
a student with dreams of statehood or a teenage girl
driven by desperation and fear or a dentist or an apprentice
at the local print shop or the son of a dead soldier
who hides behind the eaves of deserted ambitions
who crouches in the wounds of the dead and the dying
who hurls stones at tanks and encroaching soldiers
who stands unmoved before a rolling tank
who stares behind shattered windows with ancient,
eyes riveted with barbed tears
The enemy is never the one who kills for no reason
The enemy is never the one who must be vanquished at all costs
No, it is not so easy to destroy a cancer growing from inside
a shapeless, shifting corridor of blame

Not so easy
          to burn a legacy of intricate betrayals and broken treaties
Not so easy
          to spit in the face of history and to declare the enemy
a cold killer devoid of shame
A devil who threatens our god-given right to freedom and peace
The enemy is not you, the enemy is not me
The enemy lives within us, not outside us
He is a Muslim, a Christian, a Buddhist, an Atheist, a Hindu, a Jew
He is our collective face, our human creation
The evolution, the devolution, the ripening of injustice

Architecture of Pain

In America all the houses are rectangle,
    all the buildings are tall and erectile
The chimneys spew noxious fumes like smoking guns and
    choking factories vomit poison
        into the bay like drunk conquistadores
while America leaps into the laps of the elephant and donkey
    like a White House intern
She is an open wound,
    begging to be worshipped like the goddess she is

America, you will never be betrayed
    or humiliated by filthy bandits or lies
No, you will never be corrupted by the sins of your fathers or
    deceived by the smiling masks of your mothers
So who am I to live in this house that Jack built
    with the impunity of gringo law?
A land built on the bones of the Pawnee, Navajo,
    Hopi, Cherokee and Ojibway?
On sacred land sewn track to track
    by the blood of Coolies and the sweat of Pinoy?
Pillaged and mined from border to border
    by a pack of homeless immigrants?
Who am I descended through Exclusion and war?
Who are you?
    Miscegenated by outlaw blood and obscene genealogies?
Who are we?
    Raped by our own outrageous deceptions and
        patch-work quilt of disposable identities?
Who are we, besides the Grim Reaper of our own transient amnesia?
Success, happiness and security?
    Security is the powerful illusion
A flying basilica of bombs and exploding phalluses to
Cow nations into whores and their citizens into desperados

America, you are the source, the primal legacy of our progeny
The scapegoat, the crime, the god-child of Monteczuma's dynasty
You are the subject and the object
        of our insatiable lust for black gold
Don't look over your shadow now, don't look back at your past
or you will forget, like Orpheus, where you are headed or
you will stumble over the corpse of your own delusions
Go forward, go free, go naked and weeping
        into the jungle of fearless conception
Make yourself whole again,
        make yourself mythical and vulnerable
Make yourself beautiful and holy in body and soul,
Make yourself humble and proud, invent yourself anew
From the pupa of broken dreams,
        from the guilt of broken treaties
From all your transgressions and half-baked intentions
Surrender, surrender to the flames,
        to the fabulous architecture of pain,
        to the cha-cha-cha, to the tango, to the mambo
        to the Bomba of the century!

A Hip Invention

Trying to find satori in the millenium is
like driving blind
You have the wheel but you
don't know where you're going

Love is a hip invention
A twenty-first century novelty
There is no common language among birds, men or trees
No dharma among thieves or postmodern sutras
Computer mantras come in innovative software and
human emotions are stimulated by profit
Out here, the seven hills overlooking the Bay rise
like seven gaudy Buddhas
Once lapis lazuli, the sea is raw sewage

There is no nuclear path to enlightenment
without sacrificial death
No cross between obsidian and light without pain

Native peoples worshipped the Eagle who flew
into the sun to bring us back the light
But we Americans worship the Ego and think
we are the sun which brings the light
We think we are the drum which beats the world alive
We think we are the world which nature must survive
But the millenium drones with the expulsions of
missiles, tanks and uzis
as we recite our children's names
Hiroshima, Vietnam, Bay of Pigs,
        El Salvador, Persian Gulf, Afghanistan, Iraq
Fingering our memories like rosaries
O holy trinity of technocracy!
E pluribus unum
Capital, profit and consumption

I want to stop time and
twist it open till it cries
I want to explode time because it's stuck and
I am stuck in it
I am stuck and you are stuck
We are stuck and
our children are stuck
in needles and veins

We are stuck
inside the barrel of a gun
inside a whiskey bottle and piss
inside pregnant bellies and perfume
inside the graffiti
inside sex
inside the ozone
inside monkey talk and think tanks
inside carpet bombs
inside white skin
inside self-hate
inside death
inside money
inside shit
inside a condom of reality
inside a dysfunctional family
inside our bodies
inside our being
inside ourselves
inside this White House of
America

Love was a hip invention
before language

The Big Bang

Pow! Pow! Pow!
Shoot 'em up, shoot 'em down
Shoot 'em fast, shoot 'em under

Get yourself a holster, load it with your gun
Make somebody humble, make somebody run
Shoot yourself with crack, sell your brother dope
Then count your flimsy blessings, you still got hope

This endless dealin' like a redundant wheel
This endless livin' over the same reel
This endless waitin' like a joke in search of its punchline
like a thread in search of a spool
like an actor in search of his lines
Lost in the wings of life
in which we are all schooled

Pow! Pow! Pow!
There is no power in waitin' for the sun to rise
No power in wearin' yesterday's shoes, relivin' yesterday's blues
Every man knows deep down inside
There is no power in a gun
It is fear that pulls the trigger

There is no pow-pow-power in waitin', waitin'
for your man to come home from the war
for your man to come home with the bread
for your man to come home from distant ports
and quick getaway money schemes
There is no power in waitin', waitin'
for gamblin' debts to disintegrate
for whorehouses to preach of love
for kisses to keep promises
Dreams can't counterfeit reality
and love is a high premium
for which there is no insurance policy
This incremental waitin'

like a junky in search of the ultimate fix
like Godot, and the ressurection of the mythical phoenix
like the bison and the Indian whose bones
cry out in smothered grief from institutional vaults

Pow! Pow! Pow!
Shoot 'em up, shoot 'em down
Shoot 'em fast, shoot 'em under
But don't forget the one you smoked
is a son, is a mother, is an endangered brother man

There is no power in returning
to the scene of the crime and expecting retribution
No power in consecratin' lies as trophies or anthropology
in acceptin' atrocities as democracy
Genocide is homicide anyway you cut it
Racism is violence anyway you divide it
White on Black, Black on Black, Yellow on Yellow
Red, Black, White, Brown and Yellow
Yellow, Black, Brown, Red and White
all turn extinctly Blue

There is no power in the beatin' of paper drums
No victory in the wavin' of colored flags and flashing sirens
No heartbeat in death
No flame without breath
No afterlife without life
No celebration without love
No birth without a womb
No flesh without blood
No man without woman
No country without land
No God without Mother
No ark without, No art without
          Creation   Creation   Creation

Ahimsa

Ah-I walk with a gun,
With a gun to my heart, with a gun to my head,
with a gun to my heart to kill,
To kill with a gun, my hurt,
To kill with my hurt, a gun

I speak like the many-mouthed bird,
Like the many-mouthed bird with words
that fly, that sting, in all directions,
That fly like the winds, that fly like bullets,
like bullets into the proud flesh of my youth,
into the proud flesh of my wound, my womb, my wound

Himsa - the wish to kill, the wish to kill
The wish to behead this rage in me
This he, not me; this she, not me
This white buffalo of hate, this black brick of my heart
My heart, which I remember
My heart, which I dismember
My heart which I bequeath to death
My heart, which I bequeath to reason
and to the empty orgasms of power

Ahimsa
To love with action, to act with love
Towards all, towards all
Animal, vegetable and human
Ahimsa, Ahimsa, Ahimsa

To Rosa Parks and Birmingham Sunday
To Malcolm X and Martin Luther King Jr.
To Nelson Mandela and the Dalai Lama
To Rigoberta Menchu and Mother Teresa
To Thich Nhat Hanh and Mahatma Gandhi
To Aung San Suu Kyi and Maha Ghosananda
We give truth to guard eternally

Ah-I walk with a gun,
With a gun to my heart, with a gun to my head,
With a gun to my heart, with a gun to my head,
To kill my hurt, to hurt my kill
Because I am the many-mouthed bird,
The many-mouthed bird, whose name will be
forgotten

Lament

Where goes tomorrow? Where goes tomorrow?
Tomorrow is gone, tomorrow is gone
Death to the man alive, who is deaf to the blind
Death to the man alive, who is blind to his death
Tomorrow is dying, tomorrow is dying

Black is the arrow of night, which pierces our eyes
Red is the blood of our bones, which flows
from father to son, from mother to child
Tomorrow is dying, tomorrow is dying inside now

God save our children from history
From repeating its terrible lies
God save the promise of dawn from selling out her light
God save the children so old now, God save the old, all alone now
God save tomorrow from today, God save tomorrow from today

God save truth from infamy, God save truth from money
God save truth from television and lies
This made-for-TV reality, is simply not for me
God save the truth from religion, God save truth from genocide
By whom shall the knower be known?
By whom shall the knower be known?
Let fortune light thine eyes, let fortune smile before you die

Where goes the air? Where goes the wind?
Where goes fire? Where goes breath?
Where goes mind? Where goes fate?
Where goes yesterday? Where goes time?
Where goes tomorrow when today never comes?

The Annunciation

What has visited me?
The great gray spectre of Market Street?
Grandma Kwan Yin has taken my seat on the 30 Stockton
Weighed down with kosher chickens, cut scallions and
The nine ingredients of health and prosperity
She will dole out lucky red envelopes with gold embossed
Double-happiness blessings
        to all the fat buddha babies of Chinatown
But can she fill the shriveled stomach of homelessness?
Or stop the explosions of terrorist bombs?
And where will all the plastic bags of tomorrow go?
To the banks of the Tigris? To the caves of Bamiyan?
Will they hold enough food for the dying?
Will they hold enough compassion to cool
The angry heels of American youth?
Or comfort the orphans of the Iraq?

You must believe in karma
Because as luck would have it
All the chickens have come home to roost at the table
When nothing is being served, all the shelves are empty
And dust enshrouds the Cathedral Mall
Where paper gods preach from video altars and
Cash registers syncopate Dow-ist mantras
Two-and-a half points up!
Standard Poor's, Three and eight-quarters down!

What will the Angel of Mercy bring to the celebration?
One thousand year old eggs preserved in black mud?
Peanut butter and jelly sandwiches air-dropped from bombers?
The food of the gods have long been regurgitated
There will be no more banquets this year
The haves will not have, the have nots have nothing
but the crumbs of promises and
together they will all be sitting at the table
to eat   to eat

Jangchub Ling

At Jangchub Ling Nunnery
The tiny, cloistered cabins
        with their covered windows harbor refugees
A single, heavy stone with a white blessing cloth
tied around it, leans against each door
For three years, three months and three days
The cabin rooms are sealed and
The rocks won't budge one inch
They remain in this world, yet not of it
As I pass by, I can hear the soft murmur of
Chanting from within
Does she ever look up, I wonder, from her sadhana
to glance at a clock?
Or wonder whose footsteps pass below her window?
Solitary renunciates, who have journeyed through
the mirror of light and shadow
Who know reflection as life and life as reflection and
Who vow to tame the eye of the hurricane within
The furnace of worldly desire
Back home, random acts of death and destruction are
consumed like bread and water
And the swelling numbers at Guantanamo
console America's raging fears

Sister, can you see beyond your painted cloister?
The mountains bordering your sanctuary
teem with tanks and soldiers poised to shoot and kill
Know not that when the large stone is finally
lifted from your noble refuge
And your door opens for the first time in three years
The mandala of peace,
        which you have so carefully erected in your mind,
will collapse into empty space and
You will emerge from your solitude into
A world of intergalactic highways and
interstellar ships sailing on solar winds at

150,000 miles per hour
Yet a primitive underworld, still,
carved into enemy air spaces and
No fly zones, where below,
        shepherds dodge bombs and hate-filled propaganda

Even the stones of Mt. Meru cannot help but cry out
Even the waters of the sacred Indus cannot help but
drown the ancient banks with her tears for
seven generations of mothers
who clutch at the clothes of their dead
for seven generations of hungry children
staring through the crossfire
at their brothers raised to die on
the parched land of their ancestors

When you step once more into the burning flames of Maya
Will you see the Buddha bleeding in the dust?
Or will you see only the dying soldier?
And will you tell us which is real?
Our suffering? Or our hope?
Oh tell me, pilgrim of light!
By what measure is collateral damage justified?
And at what rate of speed does karma travel?

People's Prayer

Our Father who art in heaven
    thalidomide
    defoliants
    napalm
    anthrax
Hallowed be
    B-52's
    B-17's
    nerve gas
    nukes
    scuds
    dirty bombs
    smart bombs
    stealth bombs
    cluster bombs
    carpet bombs
    Tomahawk cruise missiles
Thy Name
    saccharine
    cyclamates
    DDT
Thy Kingdom come
    aerosol sprays
    aesbestos
    mythylchloroform
Thine Will be done
    nicotine
    LSD
    DMT
    MPTP
    angel dust
    ecstasy
On Earth
    paraquat
    heroin
    cocaine

alcohol
lead paint
as it is
Sarin
Tularemia
herbicides
industrial waste
in Heaven
dioxin
tritium
plutonium
mustard gas
oil spills
Give us this day
acetyl ethyl teramethyl tetralin
Our daily bread
botulism
e. coli
sodium nitrates
mercury
DES, diethysilbestro
PBB, polybrominated biphenyl
DBCP, dibromocloropropane
dichloromethane
EDP, ethylene dibromide
TCDD, agent orange
SARS
And forgive us our sins
racism
facism
classism
sexism
homophobism
As we forgive our debtors
poverty
rape

genocide
fratricide
And lead us not into temptation
child labor
child abuse
child pornography
But deliver us from evil
neutron bomb
For Thine is the Kingdom
Coca Cola, Exxon, Royal Shell,
Dow Chemical, Union Carbide
And the Power
Multinational Corporations, CIA
And the Glory
America
Forever
God shed his grace on thee

Ah – h – h – h – MEN!

Walking Meditation in Downtown Oakland

I am walking on the sidewalk
Sandwiched between cement walls
Weeds sprout from the corners of a caged tree
Pushing their tufts of green bladed tongues
Up through the dirt
So persistent are they, so determined to
Pry their necks loose and
Lift their swords to the sky
They will find one inch, one sliver of sunlight to
train their thirsty gaze
They are wild things
Innocents who develop in spite of redevelopment
A quiet wave, resisting the human call to conquer
They are slowly, inch by inch, reclaiming the planet
Yes, they are rescuing the dandelions from a concrete mall!
A blue sky from billboards, skyscrapers and plastic grime
Think different – and unveil the illusion of a lifetime
Nature is the eternal rebel
Long after Broadway sleeps and the ghostly green goddess
of I. Magnin casts her fading shadow over asphalt
The gnarly bush, the budding foxglove and
The impudent weeds of Twenty-first Street shall
Rise up!

Martial Law

Black gold explodes from the deserts of
one more colonized nation
It's not an arms race,
if you're the only one running
When the last prisoner in Guantanamo
Stretches his arms to the sky and
Israel is remembered as a great Hawaiian singer
And not the Middle-East
We'll all be sanctified

This animal farm wouldn't fit
Inside your sweet nineteen year old smile
So cool to have slipped through
the eye of a downward spiral and
the lust of gray-flannel hearts

You'd be twenty-one years
May sixteenth

Shadows

To study Buddhism is to study ourselves.
To study Buddhism is to forget ourselves
What is true zazen?
When you become you.

Why wasn't I a frog?
Or maybe I am

Too many thoughts,
Too many worries,
Like scattered leaves

I did not see the crows
         I only saw their shadows

Tiger Eyes

Shining tiger eyes strung on a thread
Knotted with yellow macrame
I finger each bead like a long lost friend
A childhood chant comes to mind
Oh faith! Where have all the years gone?

Bardo

What happens when the poet loses her tongue?
When metaphors scatter like feathers in the wind?
When the will to speak vanishes and
meaning is contrived as lipstick on a corpse?
Concepts are as countless as flies,
Desires as numberless as needles of pine,
Tall as redwoods bursting through a canopy of sky
We slip like grains of rice through sacks of memory

Names of things are like
Runners set afoot, hunters turned quarry
With fresh blood on my hands and
the smell of flesh I wander
inside this marked grave I know as life

The poem is a mirror
a messenger trapped
inside a cage of appearance
And the listener attempts
to claim in the barter
the shadow of her own body
inside the dream of her own being

Maya

What we own is in name only
The flesh marooned by its own desire
The mad blood coursing for
its unobtainable object
and monument of conquest
Sometimes packaged in butcher paper
other times wrapped in velvet sash
Like the White ewe and Black king
in star-crossed union
We carry our own knives
customed by fatal perceptions
What we own is a name
the flesh, the blood
the illusion
the sacrifice

Empty Street

Tonight the world is an empty street
All the good people have gone home to dream
their sweet intangible dreams
All their children are in bed
sucking their umbilical tongues
Even the buses and cars have stopped
expelling their toxic black plumes
Only the bars have left their dim lights on
for the drunkards who refuse to sleep
for the drunkards who vomit their dreams
because they have no dreams left
Only the drunk are without homes to go home to
because nothing belongs to them
Because every drunkard is a lover without love
Just as every lover is drunk with love

Tonight two stars will appear in the empty sky
They will rise like two burning phoenixes
into a black hole of silence
A silence that consumes all the despair of your eyes
A silence which swallows night whole

Your eyes swallow time itself
They never sleep, never blink, never shut
They are streets, the longest streets of all
Because they have no destination
They are the loneliest eyes of all
because they inhabit darkness
They dream without awakening
They are hollow curtains
with lashes of velvet moss
They are liquid bottomfish
Where shadows dart in and out of pumice caves
Impervious to sound and rain
Coral tributaries, tendrils of bone and shell
dilate in the moons of your pupils

When you are so far below
Swimming in your amphibious tundra
Your body knows no shape or form
You float up to convoluting peaks
Where windows and doorways open like mirrors
Your hands and feet brush
the detritus of earth away like rain
I float and float in joyous rapture
Reveling in your glowing womb
A burning fetus, a flower of night
Entombed

Tonight the world is the longest street of all
It wraps around me like a funeral shroud
A winding, winding milky way, stretching
to the stars

Heart of Wisdom

Blessed one, thus I have heard . . .
In emptiness there is no form
Form is emptiness, emptiness is form
Emptiness is not other than form and
form is not other than emptiness
Before emptiness there was form
before form there was emptiness

Prajnaparamita is the mother of all Buddhas
The perfection of transcendant wisdom,
The heart and midwife of true mind

Before I was a mother, I was a daughter
After I was a daughter, I was a mother
Before I was a daughter, I was nothing
After I was a daughter, I was nothing

My own precious daughter,
you who made the four walls echo with laughter
who turned noise into music
The very same girl, who sprouted
From an egg inside my womb
who I heard cough, once or twice as
you awakened at dawn
to journey down a mountain creek
Never to return
In the blink of an eye, you are gone

Sariputra, the Bodhisatva, Avalokitesvara said
Form is empty, emptiness is form
Emptiness is not other than form.
Form is not other than emptiness.
From the top of Rajaghra at Vulture Peak
The teaching was bestowed
But little did I know its true meaning
Till what was most real was gone

Till what was most dear was empty
I had vowed to uncover its meaning
To experience the truth of impermanence
But insight comes with a price and
One never knows what form it takes
Words do not convey the meaning of existence
Only loss can

I personally don't want to go
to a place where there is no suffering
says Thich Nhat Hanh, *because without suffering*
there can be no understanding
The flower has non-flower elements
It is possible to transform our suffering into a flower

When Buddha held up a flower before a great gathering
There was only one person, Mahakashyapa,
who understood its meaning

In emptiness there is no form, no feeling
No discrimination, no compositional factors, no consciousness. . .

Mai Ting, Beautiful Sky, giving shape to all things
Like a dream, reaching into night
Like a paint splash hurled against time
Life is a vignette
A flame flickering in the dark

Compassion is the heart of knowledge and
Wisdom is the Mother of all Buddhas!

Before I was a mother, I was a daughter
After I was a daughter, I was a mother
Before I was a daughter, I was nothing
After I was a mother, I was nothing

North American Moon

Pacific sunset
        burning
                with love's desire

        Where are you?
                Every inch of your memory
        measures love's beginning
                Every moment of your absence
        foretells life's ending
                        Where are your lips
pressed against my cheek?

                        This secret fire
                sears the night
The ocean distances
 your hand from mine
                Two oceans merge into
one endless vein of empty yearning

How can we have met?
In your world the moon rises before mine
How can we meet again?
When the sun never waits for those who sleep?

You will always appear in my future
just as I will dwell in your past
Beyond grasp, like water and wind

There is only one place where
I can hold you forever
It is in the cage of my heart
Where like a lonely bird
You will stay
Never growing old
Never dying

The Seeker

The years have evaporated
like wind through grass
Where have they all gone?
cries the poet who's lost
his reflection on the world

Empty is the cup which is filled by longing
Empty is the mind which loses track of time
Fame and honor are like a pen which runs out of ink
Worldly ambition is a stone in the heart of the seeker
Wealth is no consolation to the dying
For all we desire, there is nothing to cling
For all we search, there is nothing to find

Life on the Ganges

They have come to bathe together
Young women arrive with their wash in
        bright-hued saris
They wade waist-deep in the bracing waters,
        bending their necks like swans
They twist thick ropes of dripping black hair
        in the same manner that the men
        twist the wet sheets and blankets
        beating them against slabs of stones,
        in time, "Hah, Hah, Hah!"

They shave, they brush their teeth, they scrub
        their scalps and nails clean
The men buff the rough soles and heels of their feet
        against the cement steps
Some dive and swim in the brackish water,
        littered with refuse, excrement, ashes and dead animals
Old women clasp their hands in prayer
Children cavort and climb the embankment
        as sadhus meditate

The saffron sun rises over the river as
        the devotees lift their lips in supplication
They cup the holy water into their palms
        five times
Lingam and yoni,
        flesh, blood, urine, bone, matter and spirit
        purified

The foreigners sit on rented boats
        armed with expensive videocams and telephoto lenses
The Indians watch us with keen interest as
        they go about their ablutions
A boat carpeted with marigold flower offerings float by
        and a young Hindu man places one on my palm
He tells me to say my name and that of a loved one,

then to chant five times
I say my name, folding my hands, then add my father's,
        my mother's and my dead sister's,
        chanting the mantra five times
He hands me another, instructing me that it is only one name
per offering, but I am already reciting my two daughter's names,
        Danielle and Colette
He lights the candles and I float the offerings down the river

He wants 250 rupees and I immediately show my disdain
The carcass of a pig is caught between the sterns of our boats
I hand him a fifty and he demands the rest
We argue and the oarsman finally gestures him to go
The pig floats away

Oh calm abiding Holy Ganges, you cast the people,
        the past, present and future into
                a moveable bas-relief
I am sitting alone in the boat with the oarsman
A silent, bearded man with the composure of the river
Plumes of smoke rise down river
The old man cautions me not to lift my camera
I see lean men shoveling heaps of ashes onto huge basket trays
        then carry them off on their heads
I crane my neck to see what will happen next,
        but the boat moves on

Life, death, birth, memories, excrement, rotting flesh,
        everything submerging
What is left of this earth is the dust at our feet
What is left of this life is emptiness
All is holy, all is good!

Om Svasti Om!
Listen to the mantra of dawn!
The lapping waters of the peaceful Ganges belies her depths

Moon Over the Ganges

The moon lifts her marigold breast
        on the surface of the Ganges
Even amidst the swarming boulevard
        there is a hush
Bhajans fill the air
Desire is suspended in smoke
The bells from the ancient mosque ring
        Without cease
It is the evening prayer
Such care will be given to the final passage
The dead will be shed of their suffering
Their bodies washed and wrapped for
        The long journey
The burning moon
        reflects on the water
It is the Mother, calling, calling,
                her faithful ones,
                        home

Mandala

At the center
she draws the circle
a simple perfect line
to be filled in
not by hand
not by sight, nor sound
but by the whim of the mind
the thought
placed there
like the bone in the thigh
or the tusk of Ganesh
or the burst of a brush
intricate web of compassion
erasing
chains of illusion
like Samson's hair
sheared from view
our path of
inner light

Devotee

This love I have
fills me daily with wonder.
This love I feel
blossoms, blossoms . . .
Its fragrance permeates,
its petals enshrine.
Untouched by man's hands,
like the sun, whose rays
burn without devouring,
like the sky, which lifts,
without holding,
Oh bliss, oh source unnamed!
like the wind that rests,
but never dies.
You elude the eye,
like the swallow.

Land's End

They say that the gods live in the peaks of mountains
        just above the valley of clouds
                I believe it is true
On a clear San Francisco morning
        you can see the dense strip of fog
                receding like a rolling wave
                        below Yerba Buena and the Golden Gate
                        Drifting in a mist
                                like the ancient scrolls of
                                        Chinese masters

I have never seen the vastness of the Andes
        nor the heights of Wu T'ai Shan
But this morning I saw the heavenly mist enshroud
        the banks of China Beach
                Two tiny fishermen stood below the shore,
        knee-deep in the tide
                I held my breath enchanted
                as the sun cast its rays into the disappearing fog

                Oh great and bountiful nature!
                How indelible is your temple in my heart!
        May you endure countless aeons and man's indomitable
will to conquer you
        I sit in reverie watching
two blackbirds foraging in the pines
        Now there is no fog,
                just a thin veil of smoke dissolving in daylight
                        like a dream that ends
        The mountains, which were the mountains of the gods
                have become the mountains of men and maps,
                        And the day, which was not just any day
                                but the beginning of all days
                        have returned once again to a day
                                named Thursday

Changing Woman

Sometimes the circle breaks
And the woman meets the child
face to face
Each one seeing for the first time
Her strength in the other

Sometimes the circle unfolds and
their hands reach out in the crosswinds
Brushing aside the darkness which
keeps them apart
Sometimes they see themselves
and laugh at their own foolish ways
It is fear and pride which punish them

And when they reach that place
where all roads join
and life coalesces
woman becomes child
child becomes woman
and all that is is forgiven

A Song for Nezahualcoyotl

The riches of this world are only lent to us
the things that are so good to enjoy we do not own

– Nahautl

Nothing is ours to keep
the falling rain, the glowing sun
Nothing is forever
the infinite sky, the sands of Sahara
the wet taste of a kiss, melting thighs, chocolate
This impassioned century, this spinning juggernaut
reeling off course into apocalyptic frenzy
Nothing is ours to keep

A river overflows its banks
erodes the soil, uproots trees, pushes down palaces
In a blink of an eye everything we possess is destroyed
In the space of a moment the one we hold most dear is gone
Nothing is ours to keep
Even one star which shines so brightly in the firmament
Even a smile which fills the room
        and lifts darkness from every heart
Even the voice which speaks without confusion
so that all ears may hear the truth

Nothing is ours to keep
the falling rain, the glowing sun
Nothing is ours to keep
except the tender memory of
a good heart
and the taste of chocolate

Celebration

Two trees lean against each another
Two hills reach out to the wind
Together we've lived another season
The years are anchored in our flesh and bones
The old ones' eyes are unlocked diaries
with duckfeet crinkles settling at their corners

We've changed names, addresses and costumes many times
We've laughed and wept like fools
We've weathered the October Earthquake of '89
The growing winter of recession
The thinning blanket of complacency
And now the devastation of war

Kneeling now before another spring
I can see the Cathedral
like a nun's hat blooming against blue sky
and the woman on the deck
watering her potted mums
in the house, on the hill
where I raised my children
where I lived
where I live

Karuna

Karuna-ji sang a rag which is only sung at dusk
Unlike other rags, which always begin with the note *sa*
This rag is like a bird without its nest
When you left me, I felt desolate and betrayed
My security had been destroyed
I wanted to know if the nest had only been imagined
But life refused to grant me that comfort
So like that bird I was left to wander
Until that day I found my nest
Everywhere and nowhere

They Danced

They flew up
with one breath
a feverish flock blown into
the white feathers of clouds
Never looking back
never regretting
the things that made them feel
They shot up
in a bold flash
a lightning burst of joy
gutted the empty sky
There was nothing, nothing
to hold them back
nothing to make them return
to the things they had once been
before the last flight
They danced, danced
Danced before the embers
of the smiling sun
Danced before the flames
of love's past
Danced before the ashes
of cold hate
Circled around the moon
of all moons
Circled around the sun
of all suns
The listless fire
The heart beating
Embracing
one
within
all of
them
Dancing, dancing, dancing

Epilogue

Unbound Feet

I un-curl two petals of feet
Inside the palms of my hands
Tiny, dewdrop toes
Precious and pink enough to swallow
"Pretty feet!" the doctor sighs,
as she examines your feathery foot with one finger
Shaped to perfection
The miracle of your face, tapered, new-spun limbs
Spread toes, unbound by love's birth

Near the swirling rapids
One foot caught in the rock of
Samsara,
while the other, leapt

to Nirvana!

Glossary of Terms

Ahimsa [Skt.]. Non-harming.

Amrita [Skt.]. Immortal. Refers to the draught of immortality, the nectar of life.

Bhajans [Skt.]. Devotional songs of worship.

Bardo [Tib.]. The intermediate state. Bardo generally refers to the state following death before the next birth.

Bardo Thödol [Tib.]. *The Great Liberation Through Hearing in the Bardo*, composed by Padmasambhava and written down by his consort, Yeshe Tsogyal. Known in the West as *The Tibetan Book of the Dead*.

Guaris [Skt.]. White. A group of eight goddesses collectively named after the first white one.

Heruka [Skt.]. Blood-drinker. The deity embodying the wrathful aspect of the Buddha.

Mani [Skt.]. Jewel. Refers to the sacred mantra of Avalokiteshvara (Chenrezig), the Buddha of Compassion. See "Om Mani Padma Hum."

Naydren [Tib.]. The ceremony on the forty-ninth day of the Bardo cycle, which closes the door to rebirth in the six realms of phenomenal existence and which liberates the consciousness into the Buddha Realm.

Om Gate, Gate, Parasamgate, Bodhi Svaha [Skt.]. Gone away, gone away, gone beyond, gone completely beyond, Enlightenment attained! The Mantra of Prajnaparamita from The Sutra of the Heart of Transcendant Wisdom.

Om Mani Padma Hum [Skt.]. Om, the jewel in the lotus, Hum! Tibetan: "Om Mani Peme Hung." See "Mani."

Om Svasti Om! [Skt.]. "So be it!" or "May goodness arise thereon!" An exclamation commencing or culminating offering prayers.

Prajnaparamita. Perfection of Wisdom. The total of one hundred thousand verses are Buddha Sakyamuni's discourses from the second turning of the wheel, known as the Mahayana.

Sadhana [Skt.]. From *sadh*, "to lead to fulfillment." A tantric ritual text. It also refers to spiritual practice which leads to mastery of one of the yogic paths, such as yoga, meditation, selfless service and the study of scriptures, music, or dance.

Sadhu [Skt.]. A holy person, often a monk, who renounces worldly life in pursuit of spiritual attainment.

Samsara [Skt.]. Journeying. The cycle of karmically conditioned existence.

Stupa [Skt.]. Support of offering, symbolizing the Buddha's enlightened mind.

Sukhavati. Red Western Paradise of Amitabha, the Buddha of Boundless Light.

Sur [Tib.]. Lit. "To this place." Calling the spirit to come to a feast offering.

Sutra. A concise text spoken by the Buddha.

Tsampa [Tib.]. Roasted barley.

Tsa-tsas [Tib.]. Small clay sculptures of Buddhas and Bodhisattvas, made with a mould, containing the ashes of Lamas, deceased relatives or friends, usually embedded in stupas and statues.

Genny Lim

Genny Lim is a San Francisco based poet, vocalist, per-
former and playwright. Her award winning play, *Paper
Angels*, was broadcast on PBS's American Playhouse in
1985. She is the author of a collection of poems, *Winter
Place* (1989); and two plays, P*aper Angels and Bitter
Cane by Genny Lim* (1991); and co-author of *ISLAND;
Poetry and History of Chinese Immigrants on Angel
Island, 1910-1940* (1980).

Lim can be heard on Jon Jang's Soulnote CD
Immigrant Suite (1997) and on AsianImprov CD
Devotee (1997), with Francis Wong, Eliot Kavee and
the late Glenn Horiuchi. She has performed with such
great artists as Max Roach, Tootie Heath and Herbie
Lewis.

Lim is the subject of a feature documentary, *The
Voice*, which aired on PBS in 2002; and was featured in
the five-part PBS series *The United States of Poetry*
(1995) and *San Francisco Chinatown* (2002).

Lim is on the faculty of New College of California,
University of Creation Spirituality and Naropa Institute.

Works Previously Published

"People's Prayer" appeared in *Bamboo Ridge* (1986); "Lullabye for Danielle" and "Children are Color-Blind" in *Winter Place* (1989); "Devotee," "Echo," "Lament," "Moon Over the Ganges," and "Life on the Ganges" on the CD: *Devotee* (1997), with music by Francis Wong, Glenn Horiuchi and Elliot Humberto Kavee; "Ahimsa" in *Comfusion* (2001); "Mandala" in *Po* (2002); "Animal Liberation" in *Tea Party* (2002), *Po* (2002), and *From Totems To Hip-Hop: A Multicultural Anthology of Poetry Across The Americas, 1900-2002*; "Maya" and "Unbound Feet" in *Nocturnes 2* (2002); "Bardo" in *Po* (2002), *Comfusion* (2002), *Nocturnes 2* (2002), and *Nepotism* (2003); "Stolen Beauty" in *Comfusion* (2003); and "Child of War" in *Tea Party* (2003).